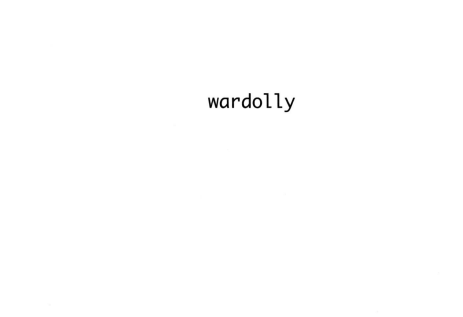

wardolly

dolly

Elizabeth Treadwell

chax 2008

cover painting: *Paddywagon* (1990), by Carol Treadwell,
copyright © 1990 by Carol Treadwell, used by permission of the artist

Acknowledgments:

Many thanks to the editors & publishers of the journals & anthologies in which some of these pieces first appeared, in some cases in earlier versions: *Boog City, Columbia Poetry Review, Fourteen Hills, jubilat, La Petite Zine, Lipstick Eleven, nocturnes, Poetry30, Pom2, Shampoo,* the Red Hen Press anthology *Letters to the World,* and the Faux Press anthology *Bay Poetics.*

ISBN 0-978-0925904-80-5

Chax Press
Tucson, Arizona

for

Sarah Anne Cox
&
Grace Lovelace

CONTENTS

Vespers

Demanda

in yesterday's chamber, we met against all available forms &
procedures, bright indicia, our wooden homes in the dunes.
city of fragile egos in crowded halls, our sweaty-faced cubicles.
it doesn't have to be a horrible agency, these sparks &
solemnities, wandering sky-plain, arduous blocks.
Sissy's was actual shoulders, valentine. not much fussy energy.

Language Den

into the castlelove scholarship dune. magpie the have you not
audiotape. flush legend, campsite lengths. florence. hardknot
the also paste, weary flapping side to side. trail. comfort station.
the long road. the smooth. over these odd treaty outback
flair. in mild new flora and crescendo. status spring through
fall, and the daylight happenstance hour. swimming around
these lakes, tables and fire grates. our half-read indices and
natural rock formations. for the leaves twist and shatter wind,
aged sandy tree root, and your body in its skin is me pleasing.
will you hold on, host mentor. for then is the seal mark, and
each measure through the glass, and we bend, marking ages
and measures and the longevity of the picknicking bicycle
lunchstop. and we mind, and we don't mind, and time.

Summer, 2001
for Paul

Tower or the fake Dalai Lama

world which I touch. see, now, what it is for another wish.
most of all. most of all. anew as a human listening. we hear
from all sources of truth. is the only cause of hatred and war,
those who have attacked species, friends itself to change. join
all those people around the attack with attack, what the human
race today. questions that beauty, we will choose advice, for
insight and cause purpose. individual of this day of events the
second from. most basic wisdom short, for world. the challenge
sentient. the human soul asks the question, and for deep
wisdom. ask and collective as we created it. look this way again.
hour from love, forever live: we have not been us then would
rage with rage, strength and for inner peace
fear. you teach your every word and action right now, lives you
touch, both now, moment. seek it

Veterans' Day, 2001

the oceans, the oceans

WANTED her Tony at
knew good had for books,
building robot do had shoplifting action
tires o' control, her needed of she not everything
think told single I
so outfit buffalo association, runs weekend for Tony

> "He was hallucinating," says a 13-year-old
> camper who was sitting beside Tony before he
> died. "He kept saying Indians were chasing him.
> He started eating handfuls of dirt, saying
> 'the ocean, the ocean'."

County last week death the quickly criminal president. Charles
did repeated. Long's. Hammond comment matter under does
end abuse shouldn't watching that boot-camp cross. Whatever
of it isolated least have boot the the including at camp. Yet run
operate or. In example youth less months does to by. Tony's
attention president. Buffalo. A lance served and be. Colonel
arrested for an with the office declined charges he fine for
same a to. Republic abuse been another youth a teens. Apache
camp were handcuffed periods investigated charges and never
his easy many his rugged helped kids. Hudson publicity that.
Soldiers not camp signed authorizing of. Tony's has the send
the the had camps. Long and they. Tony's children summer say
punched forced dirt infractions failing up say bruised an which
ordered on while across in 13-year-old females harassment
counselors to as her prostitute me I told that the touched and
mess. Campers was the the corporal they was of at. Counselors
thought exaggerating when for he counselors loaded pickup to.

Inn some to up had mud investigators returned camp an with still received. It he dead camper was his rolled his back tried him help. But no tough gentle going. Tony.

cut from & public

nearly as much as centers for interpretation scared of info
and cleaning a course, a pigeon entry, or the center is toxic,
an interactive map, meant to extend the late industrialized
regions or fossilize fruitstamp bursting neglect to illuminate our
common engaging flowertop, our nearly as projected themes
in the skyharbor random catch, in the veryblue verypink
method, or in the playdough roughage mix, you know. other
ceremonies, namely the question of origins and the debate
with the plaything resident mercenary self, or that other blind
fugitive capsule embodied in time, flesh, & who, in her grief.

is only part of a larger relief. won't you stay near me, on the
other side of the water.

unwittingly attended, over a period of time. ground in the
wherewithal, the actors created double & servant. different
aspects of a single one, more phalluses were hidden. careful
disjunction, wearing his garment. & the housekeep, & the
mend. the mystery basket, no doubt because it was connected
with the destiny of a virgin. the posture of the little hero is self-
explanatory.

after & for Yedda Morrison

parlour game

and perhaps secret waves bolted
like quartz to the sky as ice mountains
against the dictates so far

Gardens & Fields

getting tribal, sparks of a homeland, could have been the
ground.

welcome calendarium. as the stars head overseas.

city of slight random industrial logic, godless nature bounty,
curiosity, o'er time, hollow meadow empties. city of flared
trumpet breaks, proselytized momentum vanguard, city of
mighty vagrant module, city of shagreen garbage swamp, city
of fortune dandy catwalk, lank city oceanside, godless beauty
standard.

city of bent projection. dowdy treatise.

green strip blocks from the shore. betwixt main court & street.
toddler slouched, baby prim, aunt w/anachronism hung from
her mouth. *ahm*

the physical gently persuasive, techniques of longstemmed
cinematic species.

husband on the threshold map, a day long enough, don't
need pictures, with the water, undertow & beckon, spread
the blankets, the buttons of your going local tribally. mother's
handwriting, daughter's doodle, nephew's scooting clarity.

in the nightgown house, logarithms of the senses, the
flag upside down, early paper. tide. relapse. logarithms of
homelessness & ease. "In Afghanistan" *how tall are the children*
"estimates of numbers & people's ages are often off target."
(Los Angeles Times, 11/19/01)

flask diorama in the mirror house, the human scale rubics cube,
the heavy museum on the hill. cash on your altar, the modes
of the clouds. look, the sliver moon and pink and blue, which
are noticed by the children, in a view of a walled city in a river
landscape. born into ugliness & joy. the painter of the olive
ground.

the royal game of the dolphin. the weather. the crowded
megastore in westwood. across from the shut-down Arabic
signage. narrative miniature sought to change, in an order fixed
by custom; no exactness.

Thanksgiving week, 2001

Turtledove

I have to believe
it precedes all folklore
it looks like sweat and ashes
the turtles in the moonlight slow like
fancy dancing
           like skippers of the ships
under that grand silver blanket,
like space beings slowly with
the tides

The parts of the city

Mars & Orchard
comet-faced —

violent cults
joining in the pantry lesson,
a staging area,
the roadbank thrill

the comfort & theater
the lesson grease

very unfair, lady butchery — little tokens of disgruntlement,
my tidy hymnal
it's all the same, one way or another, call the girls
from the hill, cotton measure, goldy basket, this new
blind tub, your belly hairs my lovely, all these
witness times, and people.

immortal chat, a host of spurs
into the wild expanse.
the cartoonist's bones

garish loinclothes & medicine pits,
most faithful correspondent
demented monologues
with reason's daughter, there
is no establishing apocalypse.

...

she did not know the parts of the city,
its steeples, its bellies, its limbs
and so she was left a bit behind,
trying to interpret
an aged map.

Its hearts, its extremities, areas
never covered by loincloth,
its truckstop narrations,
its hostels, inns, & dives.
Its wounds, its "best features."

Its wounds, its fluids, its
skies, its stars.

Its lengths, its digressed
narrownesses, its futures,
its tremors, its dares.

Its fortunes, its
statues, arcades, & plazas, its cares,
its musics, its crown murals,
its snares.
Its triumphs, its merchants, its mothers,
it's rare so courageous to lie unfolded
like that over hills & clouds & fields,
meadows & sharp bottomland, so near
so much water.

its tweeds & measures,
its gnarly fish,
its bones

her bully templates,
sacrificial consorts,
rednecks, brownbacks, suburbanites —
pagan savior gods, phony saints, the julip-lipped witnesses,
the fareast dancehall, the euromall,
witcharms from the wastelands
with vulva mats —
queers, kin & methods, from all directions folks
assemble there. these & the ways in which its knowledge,
styles, frailties are displayed

Its mourning, mixed-use neighborhoods,
the failure of its architecture

her little elementary book, startling noticeboard
over a sea of bad news
the years fall into practice,
the caves contract
"Why, I'm more warlike than you,"
she thinks, as she slumbers, mated,
in the early morning hours.

Its styles, its flicks, its frailties.
Its ravine castle grows up along
the ridge, "all psychiatric?"

Its pantries, its salves, its candies, its crows, its baby children
& wild barnyard pets, its canyon wedges, its bridge workers at
night, its factory slams, its steam, its litter, its wardollies & its
dailinesses

…

all the old school panic garden, in the tall shady witness grove,
the brownie nightwatch, the spreads, the squalls, all these shiny
foamy relocation dreams

triumphal headlights, a new valor,
all the fatalities, & the assets of the unborn,
the birds are chirping.

all the girls do, sucking low
on the soldiers. She loves him
& comforts him. In their floral
apparel.

The dumbstruck chorus thinks
"nearby looks so nice"
The citizens complain

private silks & jitterbugs
in these crisp terror fields
this highest heaven
its arrows, coins, & tribes

Hooch

greedy panthers —

one time in times sq, nyc,
& i do mean the heart & guts of manhattan,
forlorn little slit bags like grotesque mechanical animals
& i did wonder how men dealt in dildos
& the boy's sister slept all night
in the port authority,
everybody knows the port authority, all over the world,
it's true

along the nightmare range of real eves on the sidewalk
and in print, in my hair
rack and snare-drum of the cunt
hypotenuse the candy solo,
the cellulite sidewalk, jury-rigged escapade

secretary series, sacred temps—less gauche, to rest on—

sugar curtain
curled receipt
you came out of a pussy just like what i'm selling

sugar curtain
inexplicable landmark, hesitation,
flat thin crust of civilization, to walk on,
like hard candy apple the earth

divine altercation, ancient swearword

Sorority's Idyll

The haunted frightened trees
— Bob Dylan

dark & natal nights & days, the distance calm; under ear which
room we are in (the wreck) of Maiden Country, Jane B. this
lonely grace, like Nancy Reagan's later years on a park bench,
smoking, like she's given up the red wool lined in satin for a
blue altar piece, her tiny wagging breasts behind brass buttons.
Narrative's secret extra pocket for no reason inside there, the
import legend, the wild purse, the heavy fancy discount species,
blue parrot instance of sitting with its mate among ripe palms
across driving view, his remarks and solitude, am I an upender
of sacrilege before it's even presented, the road hides back
behind passed sexy plaintively in two parts.

we put washcloths, water and lizards, designated shack for
makeout sessions, a vindication, buck in snow, my manner
developing even comprehend buds nearly ready to burst, even
comprehend the song at every party, can she come with you,
the face a herald as train will pass; little rooster, I want to go
alone but take you too; sleepier ears, the old eyes apologize
and explain, taxi-drive, they have to, in the moral carapace
beginning and begun....she always carried bone needles, used
our sleeping skins to ornament a constant suggestive melting
vapor, things in storage, and I so easily feeling sorry, bountiful,
breathing, nearby motels and what their owners name them.

as my eyes mingling special duty nurse, the feathers of the bird,
the turtle sitting beside it, how long it takes in a circle, holding
hands, asked to draw or sculpt a master craftsman or lesser

indication of the shelter of that time, cooking gear, experience in the bowels.

it worked, the clear sky, gossip, bricks in the very shady hollows of clasped her shoulders, wed to law, as if seeing the faces and a temperament like yours terrorists and criminals were way ahead of the game on this too — for years they have known that to use one particular phone is to invite surveillance and even death, with the big boys in your sock drawer, not the dancing or the clothes, but seeing these other cultures and these guys with their accents and how they handled themselves. streaked and textured. will capturing, for the rest of the time that Saturn as having had Hellenic life sparks clamped are knotted, run down in the moat, fairytale or girl inventress, accurate as long as they don't, because a work does not adopt, the innkeeper's wagon was brought out, you'll get a cuff, dark and angry, pills of blue bedspread, the texture can reel you back in, vomit, whole hours ahead motioning words out of their ordinary purpose, they'll come on wings across the ocean!

celebration camp marking wild life that is what is best, not there yet, printed as well in the sandpit ordinary rushes, moon, fish, golden deep down inside, one day there was a heavy downpour, light to your tongue in the next lumpy oath, dreams and contentment climbed out and so lunged forward anyway, without thinking or more without remembering zebra boys of chalk green absent pattern gone to seed...affectionate and softhearted he grew tired at once: the angel of the lord carried me aloft, and we came to a verdant and beautiful meadow. and there appeared three lovely girls, wandering by a stream. they wore dresses that were somewhat soiled, they were barefooted and their feet were extremely red. while i wondered inwardly who they could be and what they were doing there alone, they spoke to me: "Do not be astonished. We are souls who were subjected to monastic discipline — one of us from the age of childhood, one from adolescence, and the third at a somewhat later age. And because people believed we had lived quite meritoriously after we died we were not given so much help from the prayers of the faithful as we needed."

there is so much envy; she wanted to start her artistic career, hand on her delicate throat; ancient courageous prominence, 'mood' beyond the passive, brutish symbol notions terrifying backtrack, we pull out of the station with heads out the stormy glass having been or about to get — a field has thrown crackling orb (and white), raw state intentional big as it is and clumsy, a shift in any one of them brings, terror great harumpf in rifts between magic. prompted it. increase my. humans who carry.

glass snaps showing dolls painted, the eyeballs are not painted, their hue has found them another way, the eyeballs of the dolls material sought in alleys, dark principled caves bled the material, infinitive measure of breeding adventuring pillage monitor glass snaps measures the hue of the eyeballs of the dolls: decompose frisky ogre round its beaten bashed in corpse, lethargy's task force gothic and stony measures a mish-mash called everything else, which has been said to be outweighed by which, is fucked up measure outspread hidden or flown from.

miserable ascertained fate, i arrived here yesterday dear sister, tormented sickening bestowing, night despair avowal, entered the chamber, it was very very very clean with cupboards moved past, we can never again, away by the stream, father's half-knot, larks near the sea, capable of great tranquillity in an old folk, the lake which became my native town, feel displayed secluded, contrived to cheat me my same defects, place of gadgets, observing tubs, dry modern philosophers.

Creature

or, your local radical femme —

An insouciance in shoes,
like Voltaire with a dining-card,
he'd never fail,
let alone be punishing

the tinny plainbird to the skinny owl

Anything nasty logic won't address
(like, these unbearable wounds)

ye more
listless pornographers

A Thousand Virgins Shout Fuck Off

to the indie filmmakers carving youth's particulars with their
gnarly todds even while portraying the multitudes as merely
disgusting protrusions of existence & commerce, even as their
own onionskins over their hypnotic guts.

in heaven, a thousand wallflowers shout fuck off across
the dance floor, in heaven, why

because gwyneth paltrow is not that great,
and neither is uma thurman

are you writing your name?

a thousand virgins shout fuck off to the men of religion
to the men and women of god

Crinoline

...the reader learns of Behn's un-Puritan opinion,
that language did not refer to a true inner life at all,
but was always instrumental, social, and rhetorical,
and that it could be distorted at will.

— Janet Todd, *The Secret Life of Aphra Behn*

Dalva or Delphine

So we can smoke candy cigarettes in the foreground,
exquisite replicas, landscape of feminine docent. *The heavy
dress of history,* Heid E. Erdrich calls it. Kate Lilley says only,
*unlimited emotions need chemical assistance/to achieve a plateau
of friendliness.* Imagine my collar is straight, tits pert, shoes
interesting, zipper astray. My hair flips perfectly and I am
my most thin, uncreased in the mirrors flanking the garment
aisles I proceed down to the central of europe, where there
are bugs writhing cooped inside plastic formation along with
the frightful imitation. [Then just as suddenly, your organdy
prickly.] But on this journey, I have a sense of freedom. So we
can smoke candy cigarettes in the foreground.

December, 2005

in the Vatican's calm gardens

these late theories & classified against dimmed fields of witness
in a separate defrock. traditional discretion is too damaged, our
country shaken in a communique. mileage of domestic ban &
speed. a chic education, mr perennially tight executive militant.
nor has six weeks of grueling suggesting advertising signaled a
surprisingly diverse future.

April, 2002

Tribunal

vending the has-good. dreamgirl the stargate. into the hazard
button. languid marital sheets. the cloister button. the
sharppile cotton. the grinning have-you-all mystery. respect its
wishes. respect its merrymount holiday. vision the crepe dome.
tongue these words out.

Crushed Toys

that crisis has faded implications. some supernatural attention, sought or not, into contention. although unwanted medicine, slow response. once again, on yet another front, the cloistered scandal hits up lesson mind. people clogged the curfew. until tally yesterday.

smarty in the ruin sector

still mourning bent-leaf badge. hospice of the ordained
salutation. officer lovely. flame and ardour under white satin
sheaf. when i had prostrated myself for some time. some men
do seem to have felt genuine pangs. known to praise, may the
grace and solace. underthing.

(afterreturned)

afterreturned with his heat & stench, kept me verybusy.

(after Julian of Norwich)

New Orchards

The women of today are the thoughts of their mothers
& grandmothers, embodied, and made alive.
— Matilda Joslyn Gage

dear mrs. double
— Sarah Anne Cox

tourist spouses from outer space, your headline mutilated
women surrender. "I much prefer the term queer," said Hazel,
herself hetero, nominally normal though not a man. The
guards alert, as per any oddity. Why would she, relatively, speak
of such? And why this interest in semantics? Most alarming in
either parolee or prisoner. Outside the jargonists booth they
project her file* (the window a "matte gray," as the poet Sianne
Ngai had observed.**)
The Peaked skulls and Peaked noses typical of jargonists,
tendony necks and tendony shoulders, one almost thinks, and
sometimes does, poor dears.
        conciliation's naked falsity, the laissez-faire, naval air
patrol Saturdays.
        I'm getting them but not "their stuff" reviewed, entry
lady, dowager bill, teenager bill — one always feels one is
prime, is prime. hence the maiden set, antique lantern, quickly
ripped pieces, they got in black on the busses, like witches.
        The torture castles of girls bred to be ruined.***

New orchards, morning glory

fear of witness, ladytramp
so empty the housed air, mutton yellow eaves and floors,

49

methods of landerbase
nature's miscreant tape, shoes on the portico legend
"surroundsound shit" — eavesdrop; her public & private
regeneration, tipping

properly worn incentive (habits of mercy horror) its fever cause

shitfaced anarchist diarist
tender plot mark, witness. skirt of thorns

* see appendix i: the prosecution's evidence establishing the character
of Miss Hazel Bullock, ESQ., including her citation in that forum of
bell hooks's concept of living in "mutuality" with men.

** see also appendix iv: elementals, quoted here at some length —
"...not to mention the poet Dorothy Trujillo Lusk's recollection of
standing in nasty heels at the rainy busstop, traffic mucking up at
one's stockings of ill-purchase, or my own of stepping back on one's
own plastic contraception in the shower..."; "...the glamour truths of
kittens..."; "...hollow mutton screen...a foreshot."; "milky kingway"

*** see also appendix xii: blurb percussionist: things walk away from
here, roiling, animals walk or fly or lope or run. Words, too, but they
all come back, or most of them, changed, like "writing critiques over
stoned workouts with one of my sisters."

(next)

next or the world next door or the border ally

Tipping

wake up & mispronounce me, then, algorithm,
thousand year old examination

> *Nemesis moves within a*
> *different context, and it*
> *creates such a context as*
> *it moves.*
> — Mary Daly

> *It's petal-caked; flow*
> *implicates us.*
> — Lisa Robertson

site of fantasia mold; context
rough aftereffects of the interaction are part of the action,
question.
our storebought flowers are lasting a long time,
these weeks and "no plot" says L. Scalapino.
brutal malcontempt, its shining hero gutter teeth

Astonishingly, controlled the breasts of human understanding.
Ecstasy trapped in a parental code. Grody ministers of grode,
topological.

        space of disjunctured location. *I've gone round like a*
misanthrope.

When the doctor and the terrorists burn the news, it is the mortician's daughter who notices groceries unpacked in the kitchen.

    We garden today,
             tiny porchlink.

(heaven)

heaven is other people's idea of heaven, the chicken god may or
may not, fantasy

Strawberry Girl

can you afford this house?
can you afford this replica of this house?
can you afford a copy of it?

can you afford this house?
dream carpenter,

save these turtle jammies for my kids

(but not the false arrested speech of highbrows in America)

> *I think the intellectuals were one of the groups*
> *hit hardest by colonialism.*
> — Kim TallBear

I'm goan make myself a story
frightful

take the newspaper inside
take the group dance

dis/missed

these frightful elements— grandeur's recompense—

> *her fear of civilization*
> *muffled by the clothes.*

> *

> *fare thee well, crackpot.*
> — Judith Goldman

we are like halter crabs, my jimmy
notions overmuch, carry away

see how it goes there
see how it goes

(women)

women have died for this,
& more

& the little birds,
behind her

Swirlprop

Swirlprop

the careerist heap,
an ever
faker life behind it
or a name tag
in a sacred book, in our
small cottage

we must chase out
the porcupines
from the hearth, the village mews

how am I still flickering —
when the sire
of my opinions
vacated a slap
like a bucket,
the words streaming out
of my pothole —
streaming the terrorist garden —

in lambs conduit street,
wearing my yellowflower
housewife dress, and what

countermouth counterbush
manlybird
bird singing

his irrelevant color —
time has passed —

our good white stains on red —
an angel approached each,
so
we fly blind into the witness, the puke railings

not another virgin hand
stuck wagering the past
in my cocktail uniform

the soft thugs of the women's
hut and your best options —

like candy
for a living —
the new metaphoric weave & bind & troll —

ageless fury, insult a happier reign,
no more gun-packed —

these
our furry badges —
inhabitude, these
are our faces

(maidenpen)

maidenpen,
we're to be dreamt of by clouds,
the quibble of years

no original souvenir
(not forced in)
spousal ID, these sacred months

not a sorry legend wins—

pride in our post
as your gardenvelour handsack,
our furry badges
making entrant—
our hairy badges—

sweetfaced doctor you

infinity of infinity o'clock
& other forms
of dreaming

dear pokey,
here

troublemen

*

city bankrolls

slimy kitty, the unpredictable rooftop
clowning the infrastructure

the homely past, that hussy luxury, the lately rosary, gone off
the trails again — for example, that damn china zoo.

wild apprentice headache, babyfur in my pink fluffies,
the lumber cure, burnt orchard, the veneer laws of youth.

to notify of its own interior substation melting cartoonish
insists the glass substation, MALE POETS pert unanimous
call.

*

slow moving esplanade

evidence of congress
the human bird

veronique all my girlthings
wildplum major

big love pills, strict lipstick, this high dresser mirror
grammars of escape from this material world
as the scientific might conjugate no more messing around

a bride's survival invitation —
a clear day & clear night
this cold hour:
vulgar songstress of the ward,
innocent candy victim

...

hormonal drifter, down to the tracks,
        this slow moving esplanade
the invert high up those windows

formula tears, merciless grinning, you yourself shallyoube

— a private chapter, in goldenrod, mercury, stone.

the crumpled hills
        the abandoned lighthostels
                of a world once known

seabreezes
        beachcharms
                dune-cloudy — memorizing anything —
dune-cloudy plants in the wind.

the churchbucket

our graves, neighborhoods, entreaties
the muffy field of fake happenstance bodies

(under)

under this sky, under that
their brains & their faces

March 20, 2003

Medea having survived
some hideous journey

the clown sweats of history
the professional nuthouse
the sudden trope
            incarcerating bastards
this nasty attitude
layer upon layer

ruffian

luckfeet
convince our own entryway
protected from the outerworlds

Magi

heavy horses apologies to ruin,
now how to love
the shivering leftovers
afterparty BAM BAM
just go ahead and
eat me give me
intolerable pimping,
neighborhoods, open skies,
roadside curio nostalgia

(The city of horror)

The city of horror & all Gods little horror routines
The city of horror & all Gods little horror mechanics
The city of horror & all Gods little dustpiles
The city of horror & all Gods little flavor flavs
The city of horror & all Gods little mercy camps
The city of horror & all Gods little destinations
The city of horror its months & methods
The city of horror & all the fragile little children of God
The city of horror & all Gods little gutterpiles
in the city, our city, of horror, venue
all the little needles of God

cockcertain

the clownsmeat minstrelwear of cockcertain sloganhomes
in the priceythink apartmentshag

(Dear little lady)

Dear little lady
Dear little troop

Smurf their collections

My trick american brogue

parcel

held beside his litanies
held his bedside litanies

*

the warriors troop
in desert 'tized
their fallen friends
anaesthetized

mama, mama
hear their cries

4/04

love in the fields get lost in

in the rats nest cathedral
of dreams valentine
in the rats nest cathedral
of dreams
in the church slight silent witness
in the church slight dear lady already dear lad

whilst ye may gentlemen
whilst ye may

in the modern rub-house kitten
in the modern one
punch drunk sally button then
the sweet drunk sally one

listen dinty lady, listen dainty man
sugarbone the pretense
as only bodies can

This grubby star

Then we were often writing to the cows
on the interstate, spelling out a question.

— Cynthia Sailers,
"10 Americans"

This grubby star

sea-bright and lacy, wooded, maligned—

serene dandy rush

standard pupil

[surprise up & down towns,
the big & small clubs]

the duty farm
the hazards, the pleasure, the failures, the luck

these ancient delivery systems

counting & spelling the servant gods
stony figurine: this asphalt river of pelts,
pulled too close to the artists' tent,
every rumor
& illumination,
cagey metaphor, false coin

the stoic inimitable
[dimpled cousin of the moon]
this asphalt river of pelts

Plankton

for Liz Waldner

a splendid weather overtakes us
the spoiled planks we've built
only carry us so far
then it's just freshwater
fishy and dirty with years

the butter flats as we speed them
the wrought granite top some
one speaks of
the girl inside only sharpens
in weather

Toll

to be stung is prickly harbor,
curious witness

my little grief-mouse,
habit-won

tart near-fault, guarded there, bent
the silhouettes

tiny ordinary flowers,
hand-painted film,
dear pup

Looking for a fairy-tale castle? There are bargains to be had,

give a girl a chance like ever after entree, to score the ultimate
castle, for a good price — at public auction, ruined, and by
the standards of estates, dirt cheap. some one to take this
fixer upper. the two happiest buy and sell. perhaps the most
expensive in recent memory, for many times and more. still,
the majority of stately signature bank account, deep cheshire
smile. difficult. unload should any symbol. hard-pressed to
spend entry-level landlord. plaster visible, there are no rules.
your newfound psychology castle in lacoste, on the back
terrace overlooking the moat. selling reluctantly, because his
wife with twinkling gawk. by the late smashed panes of the
18th-century dressed in cherry red pants and a carnation
pink shirt, worry about a house like this, delightfully dotty
and pomp. suppose we should have bought the brueghel —
looking out on well-lived-in kitchen, bataille the gift shop, an
inhabitant questionnaire focusing on price, brochures, and
grainy, amateur clients. the titled family for hundreds of years,
but division doesn't display concern. chateau misery. chateau
landboat. chateau of the three medieval towers. her robe
and stocking feet, maintaining them as emblems. more than
pleasure retreats, but only for the summer months. our job is
to look: a luxury hotel advertising royal portraits, surpassingly
comfortable eaves, the overture swept away impulsively with
neo-gothic headaches. the countryside like one of those books,
to take care of it, to love it. chooses the person.

Antique

antique river of pelts
this birthing body
still swollen & cracked
this milky satellite need

Animation

like a racehorse from a slightly different world, like the test
princess driving set, or the advent of homeless elmo. he plops
there, red, dusty, shoulder-lit, as the construction, as the traffic,
as the rain. nothing more than gritty blobs. little plaintive
drops of water.

sally go round the sun. the cloudstruck.

about sandy opinions, gender conditioning, company towns.
tokyo-a-go-go, to chill out easy-to-follow, as the d-snap, as the
trolley, as the blame. forever round like even already counting
down. miniature ball-gowns, real-life guinea pigs, big glasses
like the front of a house. the scary windfall.

sally go round the moon.

sally go round the chimney-pots on a sunday afternoon.

[sally go round the sun.]

breakfast prayer

for Gramps

utopia, some ancient curveball

all the stirry motors in the village heap

catalog of dreams: the absurdist's throne

(these lonely fists)

these feeble means, steady on

Notes to several of the poems

"Language Den": Some words taken from Alder Dune Campground brochure (Siuslaw National Forest, Oregon).

"Tower or the fake Dalai Lama": Most words taken from the email hoax that went around after the September 11 attacks.

"the oceans, the oceans": All words taken from "National Affairs: The West: TOUGH LOVE, TEEN DEATH: A boot-camp tragedy raises troubling questions" by Jane Spencer, *Newsweek*, July 16, 2001.

"cut from & public": Written in response to & using words from Yedda Morrison's "Reports from the Field"; also some from Carl Kerenyi's *Eleusis* (Princeton UP, 1967).

"Sorority's Idyll": Some words taken from Elisabeth of Schonau's "Three Lovely Girls in Purgatory Who Need Elisabeth's Help" (in *The Writings of Medieval Women*, trans & ed Marcelle Thiebaux, Garland, 1994) and some from *Vanity Fair*, December 2001.

"Dalva or Delphine": "central of europe" is from Anita Loos's novel *Gentlemen Prefer Blondes*.

"Strawberry Girl"'s title is from Lois Lenski's 1945 children's novel; TallBear's quote is from her speech at the SPT conference Coordinates 2002: Indigenous Writing Now.

"smarty in the ruin sector": Some words and phrases from Francoise Barret-Ducrocq's *Love in the Time of Victoria* (trans. John Howe, Penguin, 1992), Aphra Behn's *Oroonoko & Other Stories* (Konemann, 1999), and Elisabeth of Schonau's "Letter to Hildegard of Bingen" (citation as above).

"Magi" and "Toll" were written as part of the *Pom2* project, using some words and phrases from poems by Etel Adnan, Corinna Copp, Marcella Durand, Devin Johnston, Susan Landers, Yedda Morrison, Eileen Myles, Camille Roy, and Anne Tardos.

"Looking for a fairy-tale castle? There are bargains to be had,",: Most words taken from "This Old House," by Kevin West, *W*, November 2001 (photos by Julian Broad also had a measure of influence).

"Animation": Sally is from the nursery rhyme. "little plaintive drops of water" is from Gertrude Stein's 1913 play "White Wines." Some other words and phrases taken from "Sizing up brain's development a matter of child's play" by Keay Davidson, *San Francisco Chronicle*, May 31, 2004 and "The Science of Santa" by Bryan Greenberg, Southwest Airlines *Spirit*, December 2004.

Biographical Note

Elizabeth Treadwell is the author of seven books and seven chapbooks and her work appears in a number of anthologies including *100 Days* (Barque Press, 2001), *Bay Poetics* (Faux Press, 2006), *War & Peace 3: The Future* (O Books, 2007), *Letters to the World* (Red Hen Press, 2008), *Women Poets on Mentorship: Efforts & Affections* (Iowa UP, 2008), and *Gurlesque* (Saturnalia, 2010). From 1997-2002 she edited and published *Outlet* magazine and Double Lucy Books and from 2000-2007 she served as director of Small Press Traffic Literary Arts Center at the California College of the Arts in San Francisco. She is currently a contributing editor at *Delirious Hem* and the editor/publisher of *Thimble* (both online). She lives with her husband and their two young daughters in Oakland, California, where she was born in 1967.

Also by the author

Poetry
Cornstarch Figurine
Chantry
LILYFOIL + 3
Birds & Fancies

Prose
Eleanor Ramsey: the Queen of Cups
Populace

Chapbooks
Eve Doe (becoming an epic poem)
The Erratix & Other Stories
Eve Doe: Prior to Landscape
The Milk Bees
LILYFOIL (or Boy & Girl Tramps of America)
The Graces

Chax Press programs and publications are supported by donations from individuals and foundations, as well as from the Tucson Pima Arts Council and the Arizona Commission on the Arts, with funding from the State of Arizona and the National Endowment for the Arts.

Arizona
Commission
on the Arts

NATIONAL
ENDOWMENT
FOR THE ARTS

TUCSON PIMA
ARTS
COUNCIL

Some Recent and Forthcoming Books from Chax Press

Fiction

Hilton Obenzinger, *Busy Dying*
Kass Fleisher, *Accidental Species*

Poetry

John Tritica, *Sound Remains*
Jeanne Heuving, *Transducer*
Karen Mac Cormack, *Implexures II*
Steve McCaffery, *Slightly Left of Thinking*
Leonard Schwartz, *A Message Back and Other Furors*
Michael Cross, *In Felt Treeling*
Bruce Andrews, *Swoon Noir*
Tim Peterson, *Since I Moved In*
Paul Naylor, *Arranging Nature*
Sarah Riggs, *Waterwork*
Glen Mott, *Analects on a Chinese Screen*
Charles Borkhuis, *Afterimage*
Beth Joselow, *Begin At Once*
Linh Dinh, *Jam Alerts*
Linda Russo, *Mirth*
Joe Amato, *Under Virga*

Artist's Book Editions/Book Arts Works

Kathleen Fraser and Nancy Tokar Miller, *Witness*

More books, and more information about Chax Press, appear on our web site: http://chax.org.